Extreme
SPORTS AND STUNTS™

EXTREME
MOTOCROSS AND BMX

Carla Mooney

rosen publishing's
rosen
central®

New York

Published in 2020 by The Rosen Publishing Group, Inc.
29 East 21st Street, New York, NY 10010

Copyright © 2020 by The Rosen Publishing Group, Inc.

First Edition

All rights reserved. No part of this book may be reproduced in any form without permission in writing from the publisher, except by a reviewer.

Library of Congress Cataloging-in-Publication Data

Names: Mooney, Carla, 1970– author.
Title: Extreme motocross and BMX / Carla Mooney.
Description: First Edition. | New York : Rosen Publishing, 2020 | Series: Extreme Sports and Stunts | Audience: Grade level for this book is grades 5–8. | Includes bibliographical references and index.
Identifiers: LCCN 2019007129| ISBN 9781725347342 (library bound) | ISBN 9781725347335 (paperback)
Subjects: LCSH: Motocross—Juvenile literature. | Bicycle motocross—Juvenile literature. | Extreme sports—Juvenile literature.
Classification: LCC GV1060.12 .M66 2019 | DDC 796.7/56—dc23
LC record available at https://lccn.loc.gov/2019007129

Manufactured in the United States of America

Disclaimer: Do not attempt this sport without wearing proper safety gear and taking safety precautions.

CONTENTS

INTRODUCTION

Eli Tomac races in his second moto of the day at Indiana's Ironman National. It is the final event of the Lucas Oil Pro Motocross Series. The championship is a series of twelve events in different locations across the United States. All spring and summer, Tomac has dominated the field in the 450cc engine class—450cc, or 450 cubic centimeters, is the size of the engine. This season he has fifteen moto wins and eight overall wins. Now it is the finale. Heading into the final race, Tomac has more points than any other rider.

At the starting gate, motocross racers are tense with nerves and excitement. Huge amounts of rain have turned the track into a muddy mess. The gate drops and mud flies as the racers speed onto the track. Although Tomac does not win this moto, he does well enough to clinch his second straight Lucas Oil Pro Motocross championship. He also became the first rider to win back-to-back 450 class motocross championships since the legendary rider Ricky Carmichael.

Across the country, motocross riders line up at the gate. The sound of engines revving fills the air. Buzzing with nervous energy, the riders grip their handlebars and lean forward on their bikes. Three, two, one! The starting gates drop. The riders speed onto the dirt track of the motocross course, sending a cloud of dust high into the air. They hit the first sharp turn and go airborne over a jump. The race is on!

The best riders on the planet battle through tough terrain and unpredictable conditions in extreme racing

Motocross rider Eli Tomac grips the muddy handles of his bike as he races at the Red Bull Ironman National race held at the Ironman Raceway in Crawfordsville, Indiana.

sports like motocross and BMX racing. Thousands of fans come to the tracks to watch every second of the action. The crowd cheers as racers speed through tight turns and fly high over jumps. They groan when a racer crashes spectacularly. The crowd breathes a sigh of relief when the racer signals that he or she is all right. For these fans and athletes, the extreme racing of motocross and BMX are two of the most thrilling sports today.

CHAPTER ONE

KICKING UP DIRT AND GOING OFF-ROAD

Motocross racing is a type of motorcycle racing. It is one of the most popular motor sports in the world. Instead of racing on the street or on a paved track, motocross races take place on a man-made course built on gravel, dirt, or grassy roads. Motocross bikes are lightweight motorcycles that are specially designed to be used on unpaved surfaces.

In a typical motocross race, about twenty-five to thirty riders participate. Riders speed around the course for a set number of laps. Leaving the course is forbidden. If a rider is forced off the course, he or she must slow down and reenter the course at the next safest point. If a rider cuts the course, he or she can be disqualified. The one who crosses the finish line with the fastest time is the winner. Professional motocross competitions include two races called motos. The scores from each moto are combined to determine the winner.

A motocross racecourse is specially designed to include several ramps, turns, and complex obstacles. Mastering the motocross track is a big part of winning the race. "Motocross consists of 100 little mistakes that you're constantly trying to control all the time. The dirt is uneven, always moving. You're constantly correcting your trajectory," explains champion motocross racer Dan White in an article for *The Harvard Gazette*.

For some championship events with large numbers of racers, groups of riders may compete on the course in heats. The fastest riders in each heat move on to the next round. Throughout the competition, riders must use the same motocross bike. If necessary, they can make repairs to the bike between heats. After progressing through the heat races, the final group of riders race in the finals for the championship.

A motocross rider keeps her balance as she maneuvers around the uneven dirt course.

RACING WITHOUT A MOTOR

Bicycle motocross, also known as BMX racing, is another form of off-road racing. BMX racing originated from motocross in the late 1960s and early 1970s in California. Kids used their bikes to imitate adult motocross riders. In the 1980s, BMX's popularity increased as more people hopped on bikes. In 2008, BMX was added to the Olympic Summer Games in Beijing, China.

Today, entire families share the BMX racing experience. "The hallmark of BMX are two fundamentals," says John

MOTOCROSS FREESTYLE AND SUPERCROSS

Motocross freestyle, also known as FMX, is a variation of motocross in which riders attempt stunts and jumps to impress the judges and score points. They hit specially built ramps to perform high-flying tricks such as flips, 360s (spinning in a complete circle in the air), and Superman grabs (the rider extends both hands and feet in the air).

There are two main categories of FMX. In the big-air event, riders take two jumps, usually more than 75 feet (23 meters) apart, from a dirt-covered ramp and perform a stunt as they fly through the air. The judges score the stunt on difficulty, style, and originality and give each rider a score out of one hundred.

In the freestyle motocross event, riders perform two stunt routines for the judges. Each routine lasts between ninety seconds and fourteen minutes. They perform stunts on a course that has multiple jumps of different lengths and angles. Judges evaluate each rider's routines and award a score based on the difficulty, style, and originality of their stunts.

Supercross is a sport that is very similar to motocross. Instead of racing outdoors, supercross riders race on smaller indoor courses often built in arenas. Supercross courses are indoor dirt tracks, which include steep jumps, hairpin turns, embankments, and obstacles.

There are several types of obstacles in a supercross course. Whoop sections are areas that require riders to ride along the tops of multiple dirt bumps. In rhythm sections, riders navigate a series of irregular jumps. On a triple jump, riders can make three consecutive jumps or clear all three with one long single jump. Riders complete twenty laps of the course. The first one to cross the finish line is the winner.

David, chief operating officer of USA BMX, the sport's governing body, in an article for the website Sports Planning Guide. "One, it's one of the few sports in the U.S. where you can go out as a family and participate together, whether it's

A BMX racer tries to keep his lead over the other racers as he steers his bike over a series of hills on the course.

on a local level or a national level. Two, no one sits on the bench. When a brand-new racer joins the sport, they race in the novice category. Everyone actively participates in BMX."

BMX racers ride on lightweight and sturdy bicycles made from steel and aluminum. The sprint-style bikes are small and fast. Racers usually ride them in a standing position. In a typical BMX race, riders race on an off-road groomed dirt course. The winding course is typically flat, about 15 feet (4.6 meters) wide, and has large banked corners to help riders keep up their speed. The course also includes various jumps that send riders airborne. Up to eight riders compete at a time. They are grouped into motos according to age and skill level.

USA BMX sponsors a thirty-event national series in which riders compete in races across the country. Riders can also compete at lower levels through more than three hundred operating clubs that sponsor nearly eleven thousand local BMX races.

THE THRILL OF BMX RACING

The BMX racing track in DeSoto, Texas, is one example of the high energy of a BMX racetrack. DeSoto hosts many BMX events. Built in 2000, the DeSoto track was the first covered facility built exclusively for BMX racing. The 60,000 square foot (5,574 square meter) lighted track features a 1,000-foot (305-meter) course filled with obstacles such as jumps, straightaways, and banked turns. The course is designed to be fast, challenging, and fun. Before each tournament, track officials perform dirt composition tests to make sure race conditions will be ideal.

At one of the USA BMX Gold Cup races, more than four hundred professional and amateur riders raced. Over two days, moto after moto with no more than eight riders flew out of the retractable starting gate. Riders pedaled furiously as they hopped over obstacles and leaned into sharp turns. The course took riders over a series of jumps called the rhythm section.

Each rider must find his or her own pace and technique to maneuver the jumps quickly. Riders can jump them one by one, several at a time, or a combination of both. On the short, crowded track, skilled riders know how to avoid collisions and are constantly looking for an opportunity to pass another rider. A single mistake, such as a bad start, a

BMX racers burst out of the starting gate and lean over their handlebars as they pedal their bikes down the first hill of the course.

miscalculated jump, a collision, or even a slip on the pedals, can be the difference between winning and losing. Less than sixty seconds after the start, the riders crossed the finish line. At the end of the tournament, winners from each division were crowned.

CHAPTER TWO

GOT TO HAVE IT: ESSENTIAL GEAR

Before racing, motocross and BMX riders make sure their bikes are in top shape and they have the right gear. Not being prepared can be the difference between mastering the course and landing in the hospital with a serious injury.

Not having the funds for gear isn't a problem. For BMX racing, more than three hundred tracks in forty-nine states offer loaner bikes and helmets for those who cannot afford their own. According to USA BMX's John David, BMX tracks are a place where everyone can come and give off-road racing a try.

MOTOCROSS BIKES: FAST AND TOUGH

In both motocross and BMX, the most important piece of equipment is the bike. Motocross bikes are built to handle racing over rough terrain without breaking down. Wide tires with thick treads give the bike better traction to plow through dirt and mud. Shock absorbers on the front and back of the bike help make the rough race a little bit smoother. A good suspension system makes the bike easier to handle and brake.

Motocross engines can be either two strokes or four strokes. The name comes from how the engine creates power. In the early days of racing, most engines were four strokes. Today, riders choose an engine based on their own preference and riding style. Each has its pros and cons. Bikes with two-stroke engines are often lighter and faster, with a powerful kick. A two-

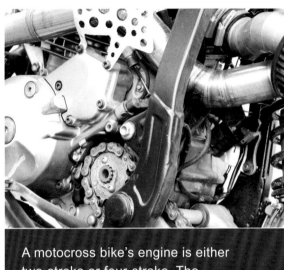

A motocross bike's engine is either two-stroke or four-stroke. The engine must be able to withstand the unpredictable demands of the race.

stroke engine can produce more power than a four-stroke engine of the same size. At the same time, they are also more difficult to ride and control. Bikes with four-stroke engines may be heavier, but they are often easier to control and maneuver.

When it comes to the weight of the bike, less is more. Lightweight bikes help racers reach top speeds on the course and improve acceleration and handling. The frame is like the bike's skeleton. It holds all of the bike's components in place. Motocross bikes are typically made of either aluminum or steel. Because aluminum is lighter, many of today's top motocross bikes use aluminum frames. Aluminum makes the frame light, but also strong and durable enough to withstand the beating the bike takes on a motocross course. Aluminum also gives the frame enough flex so that the rider can feel its performance. The rider can make small adjustments on the course. Lightweight titanium fuel tanks and engines also keep the bike's overall weight low.

BMX BIKES: BUILT FOR SPEED

BMX racing bikes are designed for short, high-speed sprints around a dirt track with a variety of jumps, turns, and obstacles. BMX racing bikes are very similar to motocross bikes, but without an engine. Riders ride in a more upright position, which gives them better control of the handlebars and makes it easier to see the course. To withstand the action-packed course, BMX racing bikes are built to be very lightweight to maximize speed. Their frames are often made from chromoly, a steel alloy, which gives the rider speed and control. BMX racing bikes typically have only one gear.

Even the wheels on a BMX racing bike are designed for speed. Twenty-inch (50.8 cm) wheels help riders accelerate fast and handle big landings. Narrow tires on these bikes allow for better acceleration. Small, knobby tread designs help the tires to grip the hard-packed dirt racecourse.

HIGH-TECH HELMETS

A well-fitting helmet is the single most important piece of protective gear for motocross and BMX racers. Today's helmets use high-tech materials and designs to protect riders and their brains from serious injury. These helmets use two parts—an outer shell and an inner liner—that work together to protect the skull.

The helmet's outer shell is molded from lightweight and strong materials such as fiberglass, resin, carbon fiber, or Kevlar. The shell protects the head from sharp or hard objects that may kick into the air. It also takes the brunt of the impact if the rider's head hits the ground.

The inner liner is made of expanded polystyrene (EPS). It cushions the head and absorbs the force of an impact. When a helmet hits the ground, the two parts of the helmet work together to protect the head. The hard fiberglass outer shell disperses the initial impact of the ground. As the force of the impact pushes the fiberglass inward, the softer inner liner absorbs the energy of the impact to reduce the amount of force that reaches the skull. The inner liner also absorbs the force of the head moving forward inside the helmet.

The helmet is the most important piece of safety equipment. Helmet technology is always improving.

Some helmets are taking safety to the next level with MIPS (Multi-Directional Impact Protection System) technology. Developed in Sweden in 1996, a helmet with the MIPS Brain Protection System has its outer shell and inner liner separated by a low-friction layer. This layer allows the helmet to slide relative to the head when the helmet is hit with an angled impact, reducing the rotational forces on the brain and lowering injury risk. Studies have shown that many brain injuries result from angled impacts to the head.

SAVING YOUR NECK

World champion BMX rider Sarah Walker puts on a neck brace each time she goes out on the track. While she hopes not to crash, she knows the neck brace could prevent a serious injury.

Neck braces are one of the newest breakthroughs in safety gear for motocross and BMX riders. When a rider crashes, the impact to the head and neck can cause a fracture of the bones in the neck and back. If a broken bone injures the spine, the rider can be paralyzed. Wearing a neck brace prevents the head from moving too far forward or back, which could cause injury. The neck brace also help protect the neck and back from impact and fracture in a crash. While a neck brace cannot guarantee a rider will not be hurt, it can reduce the chances of a serious neck injury.

This type of impact causes rotational forces on the brain, which increase the risk of brain injury.

GEARING UP FOR SAFETY

Before they line up at the starting gate, both motocross and BMX racers gear up with several essential pieces of safety gear. When riding motocross, the body can take a beating. To protect themselves, riders wear chest protectors, also known as body armor. Body armor protects a rider's core from impact by spreading the force of the impact over a larger area. It also acts as a shield to protect the body from hard chunks of mud or small rocks that are kicked up by racers' tires.

Chest protectors wrap around the rider's torso to protect the front, sides, and back of the body. The hard shell, made from a tough but lightweight material, such as polycarbonate, protects against flying debris as well as broken bones, scrapes, and bruising in a crash. Formfitting designs and ventilation ports make sure riders stay comfortable even in hot and humid conditions.

Goggles with shatterproof lenses are essential to protect riders' eyes from dust, dirt, rocks, bugs, and other debris. There are many different types of goggles. Riders can choose goggles in clear, colored, or mirrored lenses, depending on the lighting or look they want. Some goggles are even made to work with prescription glasses.

Chest protectors are designed to safeguard riders' chests and midsections in the event of a fall or another racer crashing into them.

Racing jerseys and pants made from a lightweight polyester blend are light and thin while also being extremely durable. They are usually brightly colored and simple in design. Many jerseys have mesh panels for ventilation sewn into the polyester fabric to keep racers cool and comfortable. Some pants provide extra padding in the knee, hip, and shin areas.

Gloves protect racers from debris while riding and from the ground if they fall. Some gloves are lightweight with mesh material for ventilation. Other gloves are more protective and have a layer of thermoplastic rubber on the top of the glove that forms a barrier to protect the hands and skin.

While not required for motocross or BMX racing, many racers choose to wear additional padding to protect various parts of the body. Elbow pads, kneepads, and shin guards protect racers from injuries caused by flying debris and falls.

Motocross boots protect a rider's feet, ankles, and shins from injuries. High-tech boots have built-in metal plates that prevent the boot from flexing in a crash. Before wearing a new pair of boots in a race, riders make sure they are properly broken in. Racing with boots that are not broken in can restrict the rider's movement and ability to use foot controls.

CHAPTER THREE

COUNTDOWN! GETTING READY TO RACE

BMX and motocross racing involve a lot more than riding a bike down the street or on a racetrack. Riders in these extreme sports constantly practice riding techniques, jumps, and tricks to propel them through the course and onto the winners' stand.

BMX racers fly into the air as they ride over a series of hills and jumps during a race in Portugal.

MASTERING BMX BASICS

What's the fastest way to get ahead in a BMX race? Being able to perform basic racing skills and doing them well. Great performances on the track come from hours of practice. Mastering the basics is the first step for any racer. Many core skills can even be practiced in backyards and on driveways and parking lots.

To start, riders should learn the proper body positioning on a bike. The balls of the feet rest on the center of the pedals with the toes pointed forward. Riders should place their hands shoulder-width apart with their wrists in line with their forearms. A rider's head should always be up and looking forward. Also, the rider's hips and core should be tight to start the race. Over jumps, the rider moves the body forward and back again for quick pedaling.

BRAKING

Learning how to brake properly without losing control of the bike is important for every rider on the track. Riders who have not mastered braking can create mayhem and cause injury to themselves and other riders. Proper braking techniques include keeping arms and legs strong and lightly bent, to be in control of the handlebars. The rider's head should be up with eyes pointed in the direction of travel. Riders should apply the brake gradually and transfer weight toward the rear of the bike.

Other braking skills include braking in a straight line and feathering the brake to slow the bike without coming to an abrupt stop. A common mistake many beginning riders make is leaning forward when braking, which reduces the rear wheel's traction. Another mistake is applying too much power to the brake at one time, which can cause the bike to skid.

PUMPING

Pumping is one of the most fundamental BMX racing skills. In many races, riders must maneuver through a section of track without pedaling. To do this, they use a pumping

STAY IN LINE

Holding a line is a simple concept. If a rider is on the right-hand side of the track, he or she should stay on the right as he or she moves through the course. A rider in the middle should stay in the middle. Holding a line means keeping in the same place on the track for the entire race, over straightaways, through turns, and over obstacles.

For both BMX and motocross racing, racers should make sure to hold their line on the track. A rider who holds their line is predictable. Other riders can pass safely. A rider who zigzags all over the track is unpredictable and dangerous to everyone in the race.

New riders are typically slower than more experienced riders. Holding a line is an important way to keep everyone on the track safe.

technique to propel them. Pumping in BMX is a little bit like pumping on a swing. The rider pushes down on the bike on a downslope and pulls up on an upslope. The key to pumping is staying smooth and developing a rhythm. Many riders practice their pumping at special pump races and tracks.

JUMPING

Jumping is the fastest way to get over some obstacles. The movements for basic jumping are very similar to pumping. Therefore, riders should master pumping before they move on to jumps. When approaching a jump, riders stand tall and push down hard on the bike. As they go off the edge of the jump, they pull the bike up close. Once in the air, they stand tall and pull the bike in close again right before landing. The entire time, the rider's eyes should be focused on the landing spot.

Jumping may be fun, but cornering can win races. Learning how to corner well helps BMX racers move quickly and confidently through each twist and turn on a racecourse. The faster a rider goes into a turn, the more the rider has to lean. One way a rider can practice cornering

Racers spend a lot of time practicing their cornering skills so they can ride through turns with speed and control.

skills is to ride figure eights around plastic cones on a flat surface. This practice allows riders to get comfortable leaning their bike into the turn while keeping their wheels firmly on the ground.

MASTERING MOTOCROSS SKILLS

In some ways, riding motocross is very similar to BMX racing. Many motocross riders start racing on BMX bikes. One of the main differences is the bike. Motocross riders must be able to handle the powerful motorbike. To do so, they learn the best body position. They master using the bike's clutch and throttle. They practice riding through corners and over obstacles called whoops, rollers, and jumps.

WHOOPS, ROLLERS, AND JUMPS

Motocross riders practice skills by riding over whoops, rollers, and jumps. Whoops are like small mountains placed side by side on the racetrack. Riders go fast over them, grazing across the tops of the whoops. Riders must use arm strength and a tight leg grip to keep control of the bike. Whoops can be one of the biggest challenges on the motocross track.

Rollers are similar to whoops, but they are a bit flatter. They form a more gradual bump with smaller peaks. High-flying jumps are some of the most exciting obstacles on the motocross course. Learning how to launch a bike into the air and come down without crashing takes a lot of skill and strength.

A motocross rider leans over the handlebars in a standing position while keeping his arms up and elbows out for maximum control.

BODY POSITION

In motocross, holding the proper body position may be one of the hardest parts of riding. Proper body position is more than just how to sit or stand. Body position includes how and where to grip the bike with the knees, where to place the feet on the foot pegs, and how to hold the arms, fingers, back, and core. Most of the time, riders will be in a standing position on the bike. In a proper standing position, the head is over the handlebars in a crouching stance. This allows the rider to use the knees to grip the gas tank for better control. Having the feet centered on the foot pegs is often the most comfortable position. While racing, the rider should lean forward and keep the arms up and elbows out and away from the body. This is often called the attack position.

MANEUVERING

Maneuvering a bike through turns is another skill critical for motocross riders. Going through a corner as fast as possible will likely result in a crash. Riders learn the proper approach, how to glide through the turn, and exit the turn safely. At the same time, they learn how to use the brakes, throttle, and body position to increase speed without losing control.

BRAKING

A motocross bike has front and rear brakes. The front brake lever is located on the right side of the handlebars. It works just like a BMX bike; the rider pulls the lever in to use the brake. The rear brake is controlled by the right pedal. New riders should practice getting comfortable using their front and rear brakes. A good racer knows which brakes to use in certain situations and how to brake smoothly and with control.

PRACTICE, PRACTICE, PRACTICE

The key to mastering the skills needed for extreme racing is practice, practice, and more practice. The best riders spend hours on their bikes practicing every skill and trick. Through practice, they learn how their bike will respond to different terrain, conditions, and obstacles.

CHAPTER FOUR

RIDING SMART, RIDING SAFE

Motocross and BMX racing are dangerous sports. Riders race at top speeds around tight turns and maneuver around and over obstacles, steep hills, and jumps. They must do all of that while avoiding crashes with other racers on the track. If a rider falls, he or she is going to hit the ground hard.

While no one wants to crash, accidents do happen on the track. Many common injuries in extreme racing are minor. Riders often come home with cuts, scrapes, and bruises. Ankle and wrist sprains are also common.

Sometimes, though, injuries are more severe. These include broken bones,

A BMX rider races at high speed around a course. Her helmet, gloves, elbow pads, and knee pads provide protection in the event of a fall.

anterior cruciate ligament (ACL) tears, concussions, rotator cuff tears, and other shoulder injuries. Often the severity and form of injury depends on how hard the rider falls and the part of the body that takes the most impact.

PROPER PREP

The first step in riding safely is making sure to wear properly fitting safety gear. For motocross riders, this includes a helmet, goggles, boots, long sleeves and pants, chest protectors, gloves, knee braces, and other padding. For BMX riders, typical safety gear includes a helmet, gloves, elbow pads, kneepads, ankle guards, and shin guards.

A motocross rider wears full protective gear, including a helmet, goggles, chest protector, gloves, and boots, to prevent injury on the course.

Warming up is as much a part of motocross and BMX preparation as any other sport. Racing is a hard physical sport. Both motocross and BMX riding take a lot of physical strength and flexibility. Riders must handle a bike across rough terrain and challenging obstacles. To prevent injury, riders should take a few minutes to warm up and stretch their body and muscles before going out on the track. Warm-up exercises kick-start the body's circulation and awaken the muscles. Warm-ups and stretching prepare the body for the stress and strain of the race. Stretching the

KNOW THE FLAGS

On a motocross course, flags signal racers about certain conditions. Knowing what the flags mean is an important part of riding safely. Different color flags have different meanings. A green flag signals the start of the race. A yellow flag signals danger ahead, such as a downed rider or an obstruction in the course. Riders can still pass each other with a yellow flag. They just need to use caution. If there is a serious problem on the track, a red flag stops the race. A blue flag with yellow stripes signals to lapped riders that they need to move over as the race leaders overtake them. A white flag signals that there is one lap to go in the race. When the checkered flag comes out, the race is over. Riders should know the meanings of each flag so they can ride safely and avoid accidents.

muscles of the back, shoulders, arms, and legs is especially important to protect against sprains and strains that are common in extreme racing.

Taking some time to prepare your bike before the race can mean the difference between a winning finish and a painful crash. Before every race and practice, riders should thoroughly inspect their bikes. They should carefully examine every part of the bike, including the seat, pedals, tires, tire rims and spokes, frame, handlebars, and brakes. If there is any damage, such as leaks, dents, cracks, cuts, or tears, they should make the necessary repairs before hitting the track. If a bike is not in top condition, it can eventually lead to an accident.

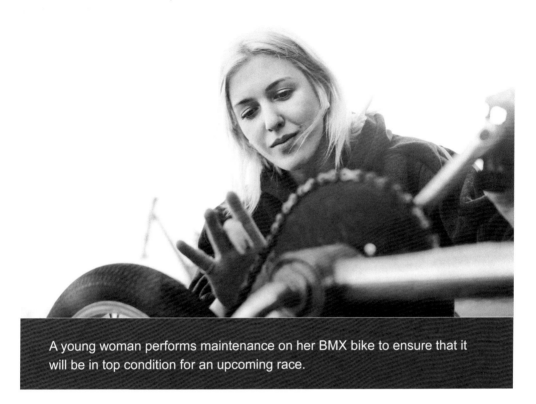

A young woman performs maintenance on her BMX bike to ensure that it will be in top condition for an upcoming race.

For motocross and BMX riders, regular bike maintenance is essential. Riding results in wear and tear on a bike. Performing regular maintenance can keep a bike in top shape and prevent breakdowns during a race. Accumulated dust and mud can be very damaging to a bike. Regular cleaning prevents corrosion and excessive wear. This allows the bike to last longer.

Motocross riders should perform regular maintenance on the engine and other moving parts. Riders should also regularly change a bike's oil and filters. They should maintain and lubricate a bike's chain to prevent corrosion and wear.

GET A LICENSE

Do you want to race motocross professionally? If so, you'll need to get a license. Every professional motocross racer needs to have a racing license before he or she can compete on a track. To get a racing license, riders must take a written test. The written test asks questions about racing rules, track etiquette, and flag signals. Riders must also pass a riding test. This test proves that they are able to handle a motorbike safely. Making sure all riders understand the race rules makes the track safer for everyone. It also prevents racers from being penalized during a race for breaking a rule.

Riders should also check the chain's tension. If it is too tight, it might break during the race. If it is too loose, it could slip off the bike's sprockets. Making sure all the bike's nuts and bolts are properly tightened will keep a bike in top shape. Taking the time to prepare and maintain their bikes can help riders stay safe on the track.

WALK THE TRACK

Every racecourse is different. The number and location of turns, jumps, and obstacles vary from course to course. Part of riding safely is knowing what to expect during the race. Many riders walk the track before the race. Walking the track gives riders insight into which lines to take on the course and which ones not to take. Seeing a hole or soft spot on the course before the race can help a rider avoid those spots and prevent a crash.

Some riders talk to more experienced racers for their tips about a course. Many experienced racers will give newer riders tips about how to approach a course. They might tell a new rider the best way to set up their bike. These tips can help a rider race safely.

SAFETY FOR EVERYONE

Accidents happen in extreme racing. At some point on a bike, every rider will crash. Crashes happen to everyone, from beginners to pros. Prepared riders know themselves, their equipment, and the track. By taking safety measures both on and off the track, riders can make sure they are able to keep riding many races in the future.

CHAPTER FIVE

LEGENDS OF THE TRACK

Many talented athletes race on motocross and BMX tracks worldwide. Some have the skills and talent to rise above the rest. These superstars on bikes come from different places and backgrounds. What they all share is a drive to be the very best in their sport.

RICKY CARMICHAEL: THE GOAT

Ask motocross racers who the greatest of all time (GOAT) is, and they'll name Ricky Carmichael, hands down. Born in 1979 in Florida, Carmichael started riding motocross after watching his cousin ride. He thought it looked fun. Carmichael turned pro in 1996 when he was only sixteen years old. That year, he finished in eighth place overall and was voted rookie of the year in the 125cc engine class. Over the

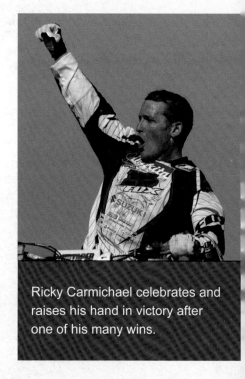

Ricky Carmichael celebrates and raises his hand in victory after one of his many wins.

A TEST OF ENDURANCE

Enduro is a type of motocross racing that is a brutal test of endurance for the rider. The race is physically and mentally challenging. Riders maneuver through tree branches, fallen logs, and rocky uphill climbs. They splash through streams and ride across gravel, dirt, sand, and mud for long distances. Some enduro races can last for days.

One of the world's most extreme enduro races is the Roof of Africa. It takes place in Lesotho, Africa. Riders race 280 miles (450 kilometers) over three days. Sometimes, they encounter African wildlife. The stunning course is extremely challenging. Conditions are also brutal. Even though it takes place during the country's rainy season, the heat is often extreme. Riders often suffer from dehydration and exhaustion. Many times, less than half of the riders complete the race.

next eleven years, Carmichael would become the world's most dominant American Motorcyclist Association (AMA) motocross rider.

In his first full season in 1997, Carmichael won his first AMA 125 Motocross Championship. The championship is a series of twelve races that begins in May and ends in August at tracks across the country. He would go on to win fifteen national championships in motocross and supercross, three motocross team world championships, and one individual world championship in supercross. In 2002, Carmichael was undefeated for the entire season, winning every race. He repeated that feat in 2005, going undefeated once again.

By the time Carmichael retired in 2007, he had 150 combined motocross and supercross wins. He still holds the record for the most combined wins of any rider in the history of motocross and supercross.

ALISE "THE BEAST"

Alise Post Willoughby celebrates with her silver medal in the women's BMX cycling event at the 2016 Summer Olympics in Rio de Janeiro, Brazil.

Born in St. Cloud, Minnesota, in 1991, Alise Post Willoughby is one of the most talented BMX racers to step onto the track. She started racing BMX at age six at the urging of one of her older brothers. At first, she refused to do it, but eventually she did try it. At first, she won a few local races. By age ten, Willoughby won her first amateur title.

Over her career, Willoughby has won eleven BMX National Championships. She has also won four world championship medals—gold in 2017, silver in 2014, and bronze in 2010 and 2016. She has also competed in two Olympic Games

(2012 and 2016). At the 2016 Olympics, she won the silver medal.

In a 2018 interview for *USA Cycling*, Willoughby talked about why she continues to race. "I really enjoy the thrill of the competition in BMX racing. I have always been a competitive person, but the head-to-head aspect of BMX has always drawn me to it," she said. "Couple the heart pumping head-to-head drive with the adrenaline rush of going 40 mph [64 kilometers per hour] over 40-foot [12.2-meter] gaps off of a three-story tall starting hill with seven other riders, no lanes and no suspension, and that's what I call fun!"

JAMES "BUBBA" STEWART: "THE FASTEST MAN ON THE PLANET"

Born in 1985, James "Bubba" Stewart has dominated dirt tracks since he was a kid. His father was a professional motocross racer, so Stewart was around bikes from an early age. He started riding his own bikes at age three. As a kid, Stewart practiced in his backyard every day. By the time he was seven, Stewart had won his first national amateur championship. He had also picked up his first sponsor. He went on to win an impressive eleven Amateur National titles.

When he turned pro in 2002, Stewart kept winning. In his rookie year, Stewart won the 125 AMA Motocross Championship. He became the first African American racer to win a major motocross championship. In 2008, Stewart had his best season of racing. He won all twenty-four motos that summer. The only other person to go undefeated for an

James "Bubba" Stewart relaxes on his bike as he gets ready for a
motocross race at Reliant Stadium in Houston, Texas.

entire season was Ricky Carmichael. Since 2002, Stewart
has racked up ninety-eight AMA wins.

Stewart is known for his extraordinary skill, daredevil
speed, and big jumps. Fans call him the Fastest Man on
the Planet. They say that he can do things on the track that
seem unreal at times. Stewart even invented a racing move
called the Bubba Scrub. He uses it to stay low and fast off
jumps. He throws his bike sideways off a jump and flies with
the bike almost horizontal through the air. It allows him to hit
the jump with more speed and stay lower than other riders.
The lower path reduces flight time and allows Stewart to get
over jumps faster.

BRINGING HOME THE GOLD

In August 2016, American Connor Fields took to the track for his final race of the 2016 Olympic Games. The BMX racer led from the starting gate to the finish line. He won the United States' first gold medal in BMX racing. It was a dream come true.

At age fourteen, Fields dreamed of being a BMX champion. After competing as an amateur for several years, Fields turned pro in 2011. At that time, he "really 'turned up the heat' on trying to make my dream a reality," as he wrote in a profile on his website. Fields has won numerous medals and trophies in addition to his Olympic gold medal. In 2011, he won the Pan American Games Gold medal. He is also a two-time Time Trial World Champion in 2012 and 2013. He has won three USA Cycling national titles in 2012, 2014, and 2016.

Fields continues to race his BMX bike around the world. "I am now seven years into my pro career, and I still love it as much as I did when I was that young kid who would ride until the street lights came on. BMX is in my blood," he says in a profile on his website.

EXTREME THRILLS

Motocross and BMX racing are thrilling sports for people of all ages and abilities. Each race presents a new and exciting challenge for everyone, from amateur to professional. For people around the world, these extreme sports provide extreme entertainment and thrills.

GLOSSARY

acceleration An increase in the rate of speed.

aluminum A light, silver-gray metal.

chromoly A strong lightweight steel alloy made of the elements chromium and molybdenum.

clutch The device that connects a motorbike's engine to its transmission.

cornering The act of maneuvering a vehicle around a curve or bend in a racetrack.

corrosion A natural process that gradually destroys a material through a chemical reaction with the environment.

debris Loose pieces of rock, mud, and sticks.

dehydration The harmful condition of having too little water in the body.

disqualified Declared ineligible for an event, such as a race.

dominated Won competitions easily and often over a certain period of time.

durable An object or piece of equipment that is tough and long-lasting.

embankment A wall built of earth or stone.

frame The structure of a bike onto which the wheels and handlebars are attached.

heat One of a number of races in an event.

lubricate To apply a substance such as oil or grease to something to make it move smoothly.

moto A single race in a motocross racing event.

paralyzed Unable to move.

rotational force A force applied to an object that moves it around a point or axis.

shock absorbers Components of a vehicle that are designed to reduce the effects of uneven surfaces.

spectacularly With a lot of flash, excitement, or drawing attention to oneself.

sprocket A disc with teethlike projections that engage with the links of a motocross or BMX bike chain.

tense Anxious or on edge.

tension A state of being stretched or pulled tight.

terrain A land surface and its physical characteristics.

throttle The mechanism on a motorbike that regulates the amount of fuel delivered to the engine.

titanium A very strong, lightweight silver metal.

torso The trunk of the human body.

trajectory The path of a moving object through the air.

treads The thick molded parts of a tire that grip the ground.

FOR MORE INFORMATION

American Motorcyclist Association (AMA)
13515 Yarmouth Drive
Pickerington, OH 43147
(800) 262-5646
Website: http://www.americanmotorcyclist.com
Facebook: @AmericanMotorcyclist
Twitter: @ama_riding
The AMA is the world's largest motorcycling organization. It
sponsors many competitions for a variety of motorsports,
including motocross and supercross.

BMX Racing League
(833) 251-9407
info@bmxracingleague.com
Facebook, Twitter: @bmxracingleague
BMX Racing League is a nationwide group that allows
young people to learn about the sport of BMX racing by
organizing local meet ups, leagues, and competitions.

Canadian Motorcycle Association
605 James Street N., 4th floor
Hamilton, Ontario L8L 1J9
(905) 522-5705
Website: http://www.motorcyclingcanada.ca
Facebook: @motorcyclingcanada
The Canadian Motorcycle Association is Canada's national
association for motorcyclists. The association oversees
motorcycling and snowmobiling throughout Canada.

Cycling Canada
2197 Riverside Drive, Suite 203
Ottawa, ON
Canada K1H 7X3
(613) 248-1353
Website: http://www.cyclingcanada.ca
Facebook and Twitter: @CyclingCanada
Cycling Canada is the governing body for cycling in
    Canada, including BMX racing. It works to promote and
    organize the sport of cycling in Canada.

Federation Internationale de Motocyclisme (FIM)
11, Route de Suisse
1295 Mies
Switzerland
+41 (0) 22 950 95 00
Website: http://www.fim-live.com
Facebook: @FIMLive
The FIM is the global governing and sanctioning body of
    motorcycle racing. It represents more than one hundred
    national motorcycle federations that are divided into six
    regional continental unions.

Union Cycliste Internationale
Ch. de la Mêlée 12
1860 Aigle
Switzerland
+41 24 468 58 11
Website: http://www.uci.org
Facebook: @UnionCyclisteInternationale
Twitter: @UCI_cycling
Founded in 1900, the Union Cycliste Internationale
     (UCI) is the worldwide governing body for cycling.
     It develops and oversees cycling in all its forms,
     including BMX racing.

USA BMX/Canada BMX
PO Box 718
Chandler, AZ 85244
(480) 961-1903
Website: http://www.usabmx.com
Facebook: @USABMX
Twitter: @usabmx
USA BMX is the sanctioning body for BMX racing in
     the United States. The organization serves as the
     sanctioning body for more than 375 BMX tracks across
     the United States, Canada, and Puerto Rico.

FOR FURTHER READING

Abdo, Kenny. *Motocross*. Minneapolis, MN: ABDO Zoom, 2018.

Adamson, Thomas K. *Motocross Freestyle*. Minneapolis, MN: Bellweather Media, 2016.

Castellano, Peter. *Motocross*. New York, NY: Gareth Stevens Publishing, 2016.

David, Jack. *BMX Racing*. Mankato, MN: RiverStream Publishing, 2014.

Hamilton, John. *BMX*. Minneapolis, MN: ABDO Publishing Company, 2015.

Hamilton, John. *Motocross*. Minneapolis, MN: ABDO Publishing Company, 2015.

Katirgis, Jane, and James Holter. *Racing Dirt Bikes*. New York, NY: Enslow Publishing, 2018.

Luke, Andrew. *All-Terrain Sports*. Broomall, PA: Mason Crest, 2017.

Monning, Alex. *Motocross Racing*. Minneapolis, MN: ABDO Publishing Company, 2015.

Nagle, Jeanne. *Extreme Biking* (Sports to the Extreme). New York, NY: Rosen Central, 2015.

Nixon, James. *Motocross Champion*. London, England: Franklin Watts, 2017.

Omoth, Tyler. *BMX Racing: Rules, Equipment, and Riding Tips*. London, England: Raintree/Capstone Global Library Limited, 2018.

Perritano, John. *Motocross Racing*. Vero Beach, FL: Rourke Educational Media, 2016.

Slade, Suzanne. *The Science of Bicycle Racing*. North Mankato, MN: Capstone Press, 2014.

Whiting, Jim. *BMX* (Odysseys in Extreme Sports). Mankato, MN: Creative Education, 2018.

BIBLIOGRAPHY

Allan, David. "BMX Racing is rad and totally back from the 80s." CNN, October 20, 2017. http://www.cnn.com/2017/10/20/health/bmx-bike-race-fit-nation/index.html.

AMA Motorcycle Hall of Fame. "Ricky Carmichael." Retrieved January 20, 2019. http://www.motorcyclemuseum.org.

Berntsen, Cody. "Essential Motocross Gear for All Riders." BTO Sports, September 29, 2014. http://www.btosports.com/moto-news/essential-motocross-gear-riders.

BMX Online.com. "BMX Safety: What to Look For" Retrieved January 19, 2019. https://www.bmxonline.com/safety.

Burd, Alex. "10 of the World's Most Extreme Motocross Races." Mpora, February 17, 2014. https://www.mpora.com.

Calgary BMX. "What is BMX Racing?" Retrieved January 20, 2019. http://www.calgarybmx.com.

Connor Fields. "Connor Fields: The Ride." Retrieved January 19, 2019. http://www.connorfields.com/the-ride.

Dirt Bike Guy, The. "Two-Stroke vs Four-Stroke Dirt Bikes—A Beginner's Guide." Chaparral, Chapmoto.com, October 23, 2015. http://www.chapmoto.com/blog/2015/10/23/two-stroke-vs-four-stroke-dirt-bike-guide.

Hansel, Aaron. "James Stewart's Magical Moments." Redbull, August 29, 2016. http://www.redbull.com/us-en/james-stewart-the-best-moments-ama-supercross-motocross.

Hunter, Alex. "Beginner's Guide to Motocross." American Motorcyclist Association. Retrieved January 20, 2019. http://www.americanmotorcyclist.com/Racing/Story/beginners-guide-to-motocross-1.

Journal, The. "Eli Tomac wins second straight pro motocross championship." August 27, 2018. https://the-journal.com/articles/107816.

Motocross Action. "The Innermost Secrets of Helmet Safety."
    August 10, 2012. https://motocrossactionmag.com/the-
    innermost-secrets-of-helmet-safety.

Smith, Sam. "How Motocross Riders Don't Die All the Time."
    Wired, June 17, 2015. http://www.wired.com/2015/06
    /motocross-riders-dont-die-time.

Sports Planning Guide. "BMX Racing Is Back in the
    Spotlight." Retrieved January 20, 2019. http://
    sportsplanningguide.com/bmx-racing-is-back-in-the
    -spotlight.

Sweeney, Sarah. "A Passion for Motocross." *Harvard
    Gazette*, August 12, 2015. https://news.harvard.edu
    /gazette/story/2015/08/a-passion-for-motocross.

USA BMX. "History." Retrieved January 20, 2019. http://
    www.usabmx.com/site/sections/7.

USA Cycling. "Athlete Spotlight: Alise Willoughby." Retrieved
    January 20, 2019. https://www.usacycling.org/article
    /athlete-spotlight-alise-willoughby.

INDEX

ABOUT THE AUTHOR

Carla Mooney is a graduate of the University of Pennsylvania. Today, she writes for young people and is the author of many books for young adults and children. While attending a local BMX event, Mooney was amazed at the skill and speed of the riders.

PHOTO CREDITS

Cover, p.1 PeopleImages/E+/Getty Images; p. 5 Icon Sportswire/Getty Images; p. 7 Suvorov_Alex/Shutterstock .com; pp. 9, 19, 22 homydesign/Shutterstock.com; p. 11 © AP Images; p. 13 RMIKKA/Shutterstock.com; p. 15 Robertomas/Shutterstock.com; p. 17 jeffbergen/E+/ Getty Images; p. 24 Dennis Lane/Getty Images; p. 26 Seth K. Hughes/Image Source/Getty Images; p. 27 Thomas Barwick/Taxi/Getty Images; p. 29 Westend61/Getty Images; p. 32 ZUMA Press, Inc./Alamy Stock Photo; p. 34 Tim de Waele/Velo/Getty Images; p. 36 Jeff Kardas/Getty Images; graphic elements chaoss/iStock/Getty Images (gymnast silhouette); RDC_design/iStock/Getty Images (orange grunge background); Vijay Patel/DigitalVision Vectors/Getty Images (black dots background).

Design and Layout: Michael Moy; Photo Researcher: Sherri Jackson